£5.99

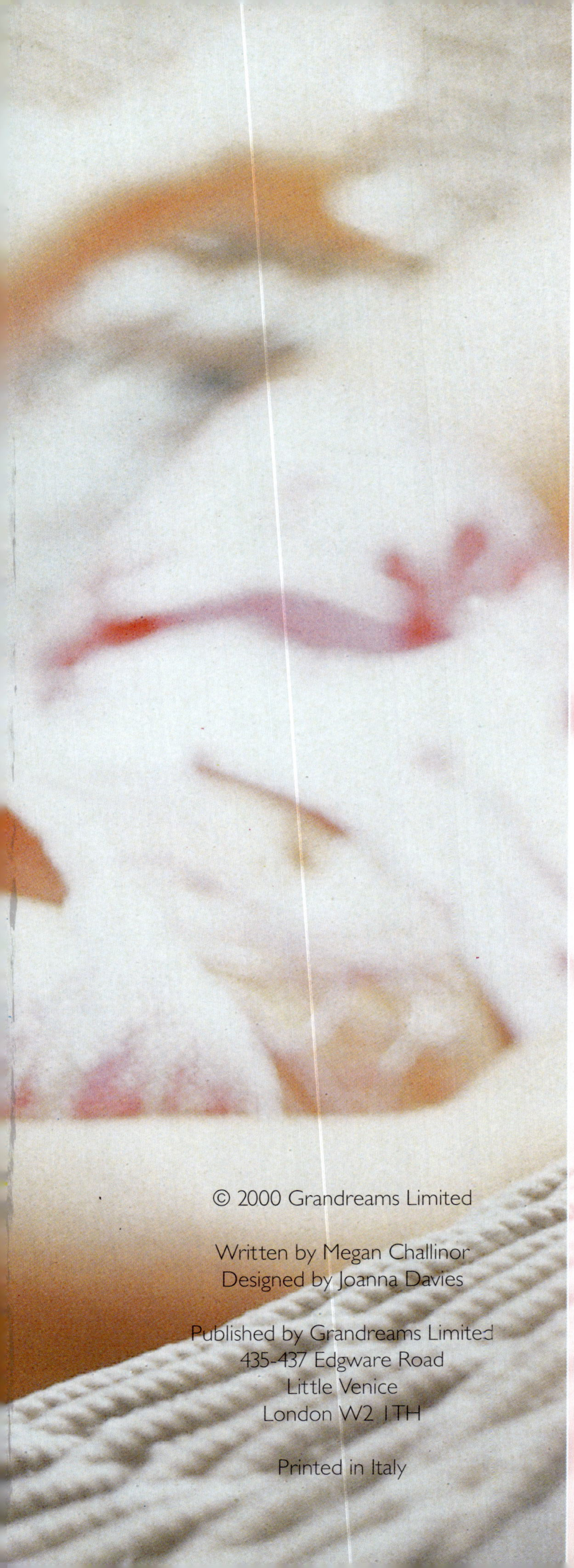

Contents

Small Beginnings... 8

Britney Passport... 12

Making it Big... 14

My Favourite Things... 18

Britney: From A - Z... 20

The Music Biz... 24

Fanzone... 26

It's in the Stars... 28

Britney On Screen... 30

The Britney Challenge... 32

Straight from the Heart... 34

Success in Style... 36

Home Sweet Home... 38

Time for Love?... 40

Facing the Future... 42

The Britney Challenge Answers... 44

Written by Megan Challinor
Designed by Joanna Davies

Published by Grandreams Limited
435-437 Edgware Road
Little Venice
London W2 1TH

Printed in Italy

TOTALLY 100% UNOFFICIAL

Britney

Britney has certainly taken the pop world by storm. From a small town in Louisiana, USA, she has proved not only her acting talent, but on a worldwide scale her singing talent. In early 1998, here in Blighty, we didn't even know her name and yet in the space of a year, Britney put her name firmly on the pop map. She made the record books for simultaneously having a number one single and album in the Billboard charts. Voted Best Newcomer at the American Music Awards in early 2000, and with four hit singles under her belt and a number one album, Britney looks ready to take on the best in the music business.

Heart-throb and idol, Britney has notched up thousands of fans, male and female, in countries all over the world. Now into the 21st Century, Britney's career looks certain as she launches a new album and establishes roots in the UK to keep her close to her European fans.

Read on to find out the secrets of her success and just what makes Britney tick.

SMALL BEGINNINGS

2 December 1981, was the date which saw Britney come into the world. Little did parents Lynn and Jamie know that their daughter would become internationally famous and put their hometown of Kentwood, Louisiana, on the map. An hour's drive north of New Orleans, Kentwood is a small US town with a population of just 1,200. However, the young Britney managed to find places to show off her talent, at first, in local choirs and stage productions.

She enrolled at Renee Donewar's School of Dance to study ballet, and she also joined gymnastic coach Bela Karolyi's training camp. Britney learned much of her performing discipline at the tough camp, renown for producing champion gymnasts. Before long Britney was coming home to her proud parents, with armfuls of trophies. When she was just six, young Britney won first prize in her hometown's annual festival.

THE THRILL OF NEW YORK

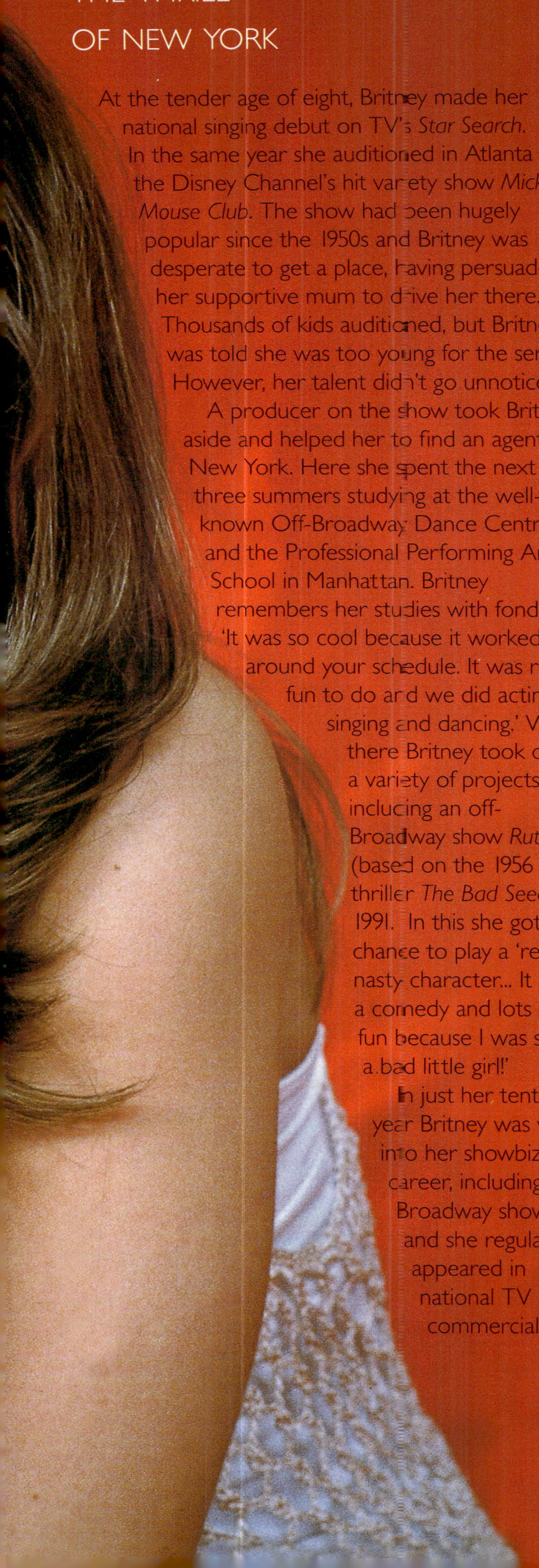

At the tender age of eight, Britney made her national singing debut on TV's *Star Search*. In the same year she auditioned in Atlanta for the Disney Channel's hit variety show *Mickey Mouse Club*. The show had been hugely popular since the 1950s and Britney was desperate to get a place, having persuaded her supportive mum to drive her there. Thousands of kids auditioned, but Britney was told she was too young for the series. However, her talent didn't go unnoticed.

A producer on the show took Britney aside and helped her to find an agent in New York. Here she spent the next three summers studying at the well-known Off-Broadway Dance Centre and the Professional Performing Arts School in Manhattan. Britney remembers her studies with fondness: 'It was so cool because it worked around your schedule. It was real fun to do and we did acting, singing and dancing.' While there Britney took on a variety of projects, including an off-Broadway show *Ruthless* (based on the 1956 thriller *The Bad Seed*) in 1991. In this she got the chance to play a 'really nasty character... It was a comedy and lots of fun because I was such a bad little girl!'

In just her tenth year Britney was well into her showbiz career, including Broadway shows, and she regularly appeared in national TV commercials.

MOUSEKETEERING

With much experience under her belt, Britney finally won a place with the *Mickey Mouse Club* as a Mouseketeer when she was eleven and became the youngest ever to appear regularly on the show. Apparently Britney was ecstatic when the news came that she was successful, and she was jumping about and screaming! With her mother and sister in tow, Britney moved to Orlando, Florida, where the show was filmed. Britney stayed with the *Club* for two years with twenty other starry eyed kids, until the show was cancelled by the TV network. Part of the *Mickey Mouse Club* gang at the time were Keri Russell (now the star of a US show called *Felicity*) and Christina Aguilera. Britney loved being a part of the show and missed both her friends and the early morning walk through Disney World to get to the studio.

Returning to Louisiana, Britney found herself back in Kentwood with a year of 'ordinary' teenage life. Britney says that high school was fun, but she didn't miss it. At the age of 14, she soon got itchy feet and longed to perform, 'I was bored out of my mind, I really wanted to get out again and see the world.' Not that her training had stopped completely. She had enrolled at the Park Lane Academy in a nearby town called McComb.

NEW YORK, NEW YORK

Britney felt the magnet of New York and wanted to pursue her dream of becoming a singer, 'It's what I wanted to do since I was very little.' She pestered her parents to contact the New York entertainment lawyer, Larry Rudolph, who Britney had worked with before. Six weeks later he contacted her family and asked them to send a tape of Britney singing. With her lawyer's help, Britney got an audition for an all-girl band, Innosense. Unluckily for them, Britney outshone the rest and it was suggested that she should pursue a solo career. As her lawyer saw it, there was a noticeable lack of talented single-girl singers in the US. Britney was back on track.

Meanwhile, Britney was continuing her school studies with tutors while her demo tape was sent to Jive Records, home of Backstreeters AJ, Nick, Kevin, Brian and Howie. Jeff Fenster instantly recognised talent and arranged for Britney to meet the record company executives in person. So, at the age of 15,

Britney nervously performed in front of twelve bigwigs from the music industry in a bid to impress. Singing Whitney Houston's *I Have Nothing* Britney did the job perfectly and they signed her up for their label immediately. Britney was officially a Jive Records artist. She was promptly whisked off to Sweden to team up with Max Martin, once the member of a heavy metal band called It's Alive, and more recently writer and producer of many Backstreet singles.

JIVE TALKING

This is where Britney's association with the Backstreets began. Jive records promoted Britney's songs by including them on a CD sampler and offered free previews of her video to anyone who requested the Boys' *I'll Never Break Your Heart* video on the music channel The Box. Working for both artists at the same time, Jive also managed to secure Britney a slot beside the boys on the *Sabrina the Teenage Witch* soundtrack. Britney's face was soon appearing in US teen magazines *Superteen*, *Bop*, *Teen Machine* and *Teen People*. Enlisting the help of Johnny and Donna Wright who used to manage the Backstreets, Britney was well on her way to stardom...

Britney PASSPORT

First names: Britney Jean

Born: 2 December 1981

Starsign: Sagittarius

Home: Kentwood, Louisiana, USA

Height: 5 ft 5 in

Weight: 105 lb

Eye colour: Brown

Hair colour: Brown (mostly!)

Siblings: Bryan and Jamie Lynn

Hobbies: Travelling, performing and, of course, shopping

First job: Disney Channel's *Mickey Mouse Club*

Worst habit: Biting finger nails, 'especially just before a show when I'm nervous' and using the phone too much!

MAKING IT BIG

Once Britney had signed with Jive Records, her career launched forward at a pace of knots. Jeff Fenster, who showed great faith in his young new signing, not only introduced Britney to Max Martin, famous writer/producer, but also Eric Foster White, who has worked with countless international stars including Whitney Houston.

IN THE STUDIO

Jive Records wasted no time and the spring of 1998 saw Britney in Stockholm, Sweden, recording her first album with Max Martin. Originally the intention was for the pair to work together on just a couple of tracks, but they gelled immediately and a couple of tracks led to a number of hits including *Baby One More Time*, *(You Drive Me) Crazy* and *I Will Be There*. Martin was keen to let Britney express herself and when putting the final touches to the tracks, Britney made a fair share of the decisions on lyrics and musical style.

Back in the US, Britney worked with Eric Foster White on the rest of the album in New Jersey. Britney was excited at her rapid progress in the pop world. She commented at the time, 'I know I've had to give up some things to do this... At home two years ago, we'd do the same stuff each weekend – that's wonderful if you love what you're doing, but I'd much rather be doing this!'

ON THE ROAD

In the autumn of 1998, Britney and her two dancers went on a promotional tour of US shopping malls. She met with audiences after each show and distributed all the Britney info a new fan could need. Radio shows followed and Britney charmed the all DJs with her innocent and down-to-earth nature.

Her first major tour was as support for 'N Sync, who were impressed with her talent and style. Britney was delighted at the opportunity. As well as a great chance to spread her name and do what she enjoys most – performing – she was also able to meet up with old friends, ex-Mouseketeers JC Chasez and Justin Timberlake. The US tour with the boys lasted three months, from November 1998 to January '99.

The publicity for the tour worked well. When Britney's first single was released, it flew out of the record shops. *Baby One More Time*, the single (and title track of the album), shot to number one in the US. The album too made the number one slot in the American Billboard charts. Britney had made history – she was the first (and youngest) female artist to have both her first single and first album go to the top slot in the same week in the US. Canada also made Britney their number one album artist.

SUCCESS

Baby One More Time had originally been written by Max Martin with the Backstreets in mind. Britney took over, did it justice, and was elated when her lawyer and president of the record company gave her the call announcing her success. Within just a few weeks, over a million copies had been sold worldwide. In February, Britney's record company released the first single in the UK. *Baby One More Time* sold 464,000 copies in the first week alone and shot straight to number one, holding off the big names such as Blur and Whitney Houston.

With one major hit behind her, Britney's record company knew that to fend off critics claiming her to be a 'one hit wonder' they had to release another single soon. The answer came in the form of *Sometimes*. The single was ready, but a severe blow was to strike Britney. While rehearsing for the video, she twisted her knee so badly that she was whisked off to New Orleans Doctor's Hospital for an operation. This put Britney out of action for four weeks. Despite her disappointment at cancelling a promotional tour of Europe, Britney got the rest she deserved after an incredibly hectic year. With the tour cancelled and the video for *Sometimes* on hold, all Britney could do was hobble around on her crutches. Her injury also meant she missed the prestigious Grammy Awards at which she had been chosen to present an award. Instead she presented the award by video link and partied away at home.

Eventually the video was recorded and proved a great success – the single reached number three in the UK charts. Within a couple of months *(You Drive Me) Crazy* gave Britney her third top ten hit of the year. She had made it big time!

MY FAVOURITE THINGS

So just what gets Britney going? Read on to discover her favourite things in the world...

Fave holiday destination... Hawaii

Fave designers... Betsey Johnson, Calvin Klein, Donna Karan, Bebe

Fave store... The Gap

Fave pastime... Shopping 'It really makes me happy... When I actually get a chance to shop for myself (Britney usually has a stylist to get her clothes) it's really great'

Fave actors... Ben Affleck, Tom Cruise, Brad Pitt

Fave actress... Drew Barrymore

Fave films... *American Pie* – Britney thought it was 'hilarious', *My Best Friend's Wedding*, *Steel Magnolias*

Fave songs... include *Girls Just Wanna Have Fun* by Cyndi Lauper, *Torn* by Natalie Imbruglia and *Brown Eyed Girl* by Van Morrison, and anything by Lauryn Hill and Mary J Blige

Fave TV show... *Friends*, her favourite character in the show is 'Phoebe, she's so ditzy!'

Fave perfume... Angel by Thierry Mugler

Fave food... Naughty but nice, cookie dough ice cream!

Fave colour... Blue

Favourite sport... Basketball, tennis, golf

BRITNEY: FROM A - Z

A is for Angel, one of Britney's favourite perfumes by Thierry Mugler.

B is for Brad Pitt. Britney keeps a picture of him on her fridge and admits to kissing it every morning!

C is for Coffee. Britney says she always has to drink it first thing in the morning, otherwise she'd never get going!

D is for Disco, the kind of music Britney likes best.

E is for English. This was Britney's favourite school subject – yes, she still had to keep up with her studies, even while touring!

F is for Fun Fairs. Britney loves them – one of her favourite spots is Coney Island, New York.

G is for Gymnastics. When Britney was a little girl she kept a balance beam in the middle of her lounge to practise her gymnastics.

H is for Hairdryer. One item Britney can't be without. This was especially true in the days when her hair was longer, and she apparently kept everybody waiting for hours while she dried it!

I is for Ice cream. Britney is a confirmed cookie dough 'ice creamoholic'!

J is for Justin. Justin Timberlake is one of Britney's oldest buddies in the showbiz world. She worked with him on the US Disney TV show *The Mickey Mouse Club*.

K is for Kentwood, Louisiana... a small town, but home to a big name.

L is for Leonardo DiCaprio – one guy Britney definitely wouldn't mind working with in the future.

M is for Mouseketeer! Britney landed a part as a Mouseketeer on the *The Mickey Mouse Club* when she was just eleven.

N is for 'N Sync. Britney went on tour with 'N Sync early in her career. She also enlisted the help of their management team, Johnny and Donna Wright.

O is for Off-Broadway Dance Centre, where Britney took classes in New York after the initial rejection from the *Mickey Mouse Club*. The classes prepared her for a career in showbusiness.

P is for Power Rangers. Believe it or not, this could have been Britney's fate in her very first video. The plan was to feature Power Rangers type animated characters. Thank goodness Britney put her foot down!

Q is for Queuing. Whether you like it or not, undoubtedly this is what you'll be doing when Britney announces her next tour dates.

R is for Ruthless, the 1991 'off-Broadway' stage show in which Britney starred as 'this really bad child who seems sweet, but is evil too.'

S is for Spice. Britney says her favourite is Baby Spice!

T is for Trainers. Britney is most relaxed in trainers, t-shirts and sweat pants.

U is for University. Britney's fame has reached the top of the education scale. She has even been included in lectures about pop music, entitled 'Don't Stop Til You Get Enough: Consuming Pop Music'.

V is for Video. Britney's first video release was called *Time Out*. It included exclusive home photos, a personal interview and behind-the-scenes footage of Britney in the studio and at video shoots.

W is for William, the Prince who is a real fan of Britney. Of course she was delighted at receiving a letter from him inviting her to get in touch next time she's in England!

X is for X-rays. When Britney dislocated her left leg during rehearsal for the *Sometimes* video, she was whisked away for x-rays at the hospital. Three weeks later, when her leg seemed no better, she was having x-rays again and this time surgery was called for. Result – six weeks of rest and an unhappy Britney.

Y is for You, the fans who keep Britney at the top of the charts.

Z is for Zodiac sign and Britney's a Sagittarius. True to her sign, she is confident and ready to take on the world... well, just the pop world for now.

THE MUSIC BIZ

When it boils down to it, for Britney it's the music and performing that counts. Even as a small child, Britney was surrounded by music and loyally sang gospel tunes in her local church choir in Kentwood every Sunday. Since her career has developed, Britney has been very lucky: she's worked with the hottest names in the music biz and has always had a supportive record company and, of course, family.

Britney says that, since early childhood, she's wanted to be a singer, to perform and to travel. Little did she know then of the long haul that touring can sometimes be.

'Seeing the audience's reaction when you're performing on stage is the best thing about this job'

Between 8 March and 9 April 1999, Britney played at 22 different venues in the US, including the Freedom Hall, Louisville, the Pyramid in Memphis and then down to the American Airlines Arena in Miami, Florida. Now that's a huge undertaking! 'It's not all glamour,' says Britney, 'people don't see the behind the scenes stuff... when you do a show sometimes you have only 30 minutes to be ready and that's after a day of press.' Phew!

As expected, the tour went down a storm and Britney was in her element. 'Being there with all those people is the most adrenalin-filled best feeling in the world... You realise they know all the words to your songs and they're screaming for you.' Opening acts for the show were Bosson, the male Swedish singer, who certainly gained himself a few more thousand fans and DREAM, the all girl teen group.

It certainly sounds like a ball when Britney goes on tour. As well as her support bands to hang out with, Britney has plenty of fun with the dancers from her set. On stage they often get up to pranks and make Britney laugh. 'Once they suddenly decided to go crazy and started making all these weird gestures in front of me. I just pulled off my headset and cracked up.' Unfortunately for Britney, she never gets her own back – she's too busy concentrating on her singing and her own dance moves.

When Britney embarks on touring or promotional work in Europe, she knows the travelling will take up the majority of her time. She says that at first the idea of flying was one she dreaded, but now she loves it. The reason being – it's the best chance she gets for a good long sleep! Britney admits that when she's tired she does get very emotional and tearful. One such incident happened when, tired with jet lag, Britney's headset repeatedly was falling off just prior to a show. Result: 'I just started to cry, I didn't even know what the time was.' Time to take a good look at the schedule I should say!

RECORDING

Whilst Britney was recording her first album she soon realised how much hard work was involved, 'but it was fun and I got to work with incredibly talented people.'

Britney worked on her second album in Sweden with producer Robert John Lange, (who is, incidentally, Shania Twain's husband). The UK production duo Shanks & Bigfoot – more famous for their dance sounds, like the number one hit *Sweet Like Chocolate* – also took part. Britney's album, released in the early part of 2000, included new material as well as *Walk on By*, a remix of an early '60s classic. Britney told her fans how the new album was more mature than the first: 'I feel I am expressing myself better.'

RECOGNITION

Britney won all four awards that she was nominated for at the '99 MTV Europe Music Awards, namely Best Female, Best Pop, Best Breakthrough and Best Song of 1999. This was something of an achievement as Britney beat the all-time record for winning more awards than any other artist. Britney also won the People's Choice award for Favourite International artist at Canada's MuchMusic Awards. Britney remembers her first award show and how excited and in awe she was. Now a regular award winner, she says she feeds off different performances and new challenges.

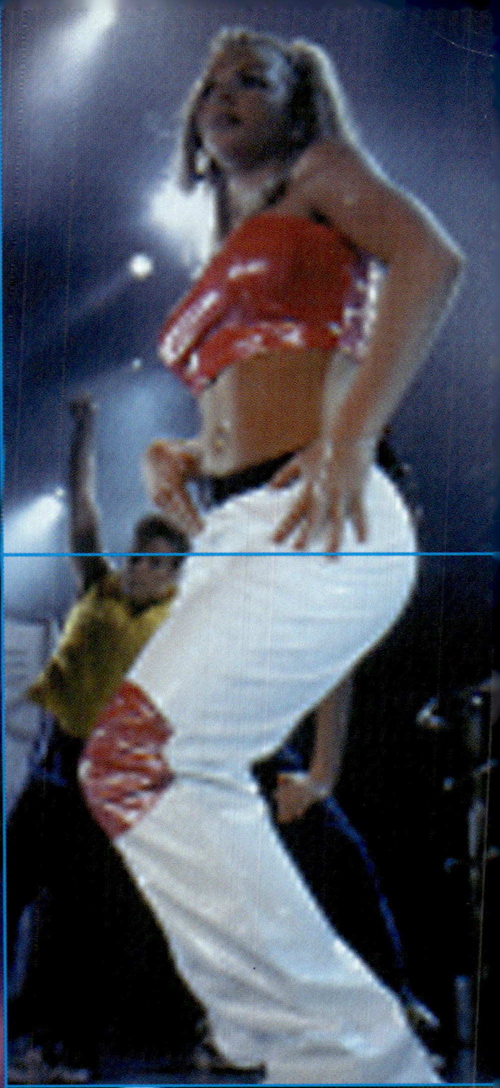

FANZONE

Britney is well aware that it's the fans that have put her where she is today. Once Jive Records recognised her talent, it was the record-buying public who put Britney on top of the charts and made her an award winner over and over again.

Britney got her first true taste of how frenzied an adoring audience can be when she toured as the opening act for N'Sync. 'Some of the screaming girls are unreal,' she said at the time. 'I would never dream of doing some of the things the girls do. It's so bizarre!'

Britney loves being at home and understandably this is where most of her fans are. 'If I go to a mall there, people are everywhere,' says Britney of her eager followers. In other parts of the US, like the big cities of LA and New York, Britney says the attention is not quite so overbearing.

Part of Britney's huge fan following in Britain includes Prince William. Britney was well chuffed to hear the news and immediately sent him a copy of her album and some photographs!

Britney is always chirpy and delighted to meet with her fans. Well, almost always. Everybody needs their space and Britney recalls one incident at the airport when she was trying to sort something out and she was beseiged by fans. Britney was upset to find the disgruntled fans started calling her names when she asked them to wait a few moments. Now that's the hard part of fame – so give Britney some space!

Unwanted publicity goes with the job of being a pop star – unfortunately. Recognising that a lot of her fans are young girls, Britney remembers how hurt she felt when the press first started rumours. 'It gets really tough, but you soon learn to ignore them I know I'm a role model for a lot of people and I'd never do anything to jeopardise that.'

Britney mania is such that she is also now a hit in the toy shops. As early as October 1999, a Britney doll was launched in the US and instantly became one of the biggest selling celebrity dolls. There are six different dolls featuring Britney in different outfits in 'The Concert Collection' and 'The Video Collection'.

IT'S IN THE STARS

Born on 2 December, Britney falls under the star sign of Sagittarius. True to her sign Britney is cool, confident and ready for action. Sagittarians tend to like taking initiative and aren't easily tied down, so it would take a very special partner to keep Britney rooted to the spot. As a best friend or a love interest, just how well would you get along with Britney? Look for the star sign of your birthday and read on...

Sagittarius & Capricorn
(Dec 22 - Jan 20)
Capricorns are very often workaholics and ambitious, so you and Britney could work very well together. In fact, there'd be no stopping you! However, don't forget, everyone needs a little 'time out' sometimes.

Sagittarius & Aquarius
(Jan 21 - Feb 19)
The water carrier of the zodiac isn't in the least wet. Outgoing and style conscious, you and Britney would have a great night out together.

Sagittarius & Pisces
(Feb 20 - Mar 20)
Creative, caring and thoughtful, Pisceans make great soul mates. I'm sure Britney would see you as a reliable and treasured friend.

Sagittarius & Aries
(Mar 21 - Apr 20)
Those with the sign of the ram are full of confidence and usually very ambitious. Perhaps you could swap notes with Britney?!

Sagittarius & Taurus
(Apr 21 - May 21)
Dependable Taureans are also true romantics and can be one of the hottest signs of the zodiac. Not afraid to show their true emotions, Britney would certainly appreciate your honesty and a genuine romance.

Sagittarius & Gemini
(May 22 - June 22)
Highly-strung Geminis are usually compulsive communicators – in other words, they like a good chat. Undoubtly you could gossip to Britney for hours, adding to the usual phone bill crisis! However, take caution, in other areas you are complete opposites, so in a serious relationship, you could either have won gold or committed a stormy disaster.

Sagittarius & Cancer
(June 23 - Jul 23)
Cancerians might be ruled by the moon, but rules are strictly not your scene. Having a somewhat erratic influence, you crave freedom. Nothing wrong with that, but don't forget who your friends are!

Sagittarius & Leo
(Jul 24 - Aug 23)
Ever popular and always up for a party, Leos can be flirtatious and attention-seeking, so as a mate Britney would love to party with you. In the romance stakes, watch out, Britney might not take too kindly to a flirt!

Sagittarius & Virgo
(Aug 24 - Sep 23)
Another good 'communicator' sign and renowned for their hearts of gold, Virgos could provide the perfect mate for Britney, just watch the phone bill!

Sagittarius & Libra
(Sep 24 - Oct 23)
Typically the devoted partner, could you cope with a girlfriend who was in the USA one day, the UK the next and goodness knows where next week? Libran hearts take a long time to recover from emotional disappointment, so don't fall head over heels too fast.

Sagittarius & Scorpio
(Oct 24 - Nov 22)
Full of confidence, Scorpios have no trouble making friends. Just be in the right place at the right time to make your new friend Britney. Just be sure your temperamental side doesn't spoil the fun!

Sagittarius & Sagittarius
(Nov 23 - Dec 21)
If you prove as independent as Britney, then you'd certainly have to come to an arrangement to find 'special time' together. Both of you are unlikely to stay in one place for long, however, true hearts will always get back together in the end.

BRITNEY ON SCREEN

It's no secret that Britney loves to perform. From a very young age, she yearned to be on stage or on TV, initially in the much loved *Mickey Mouse Club*. Her dream came true when she finally got a place over thousands of hopefuls when she was eleven. Since then, she's appeared in countless advertisements, videos and more recently guest appearing in well known TV shows.

When Britney came to make her first video for *Baby One More Time*, she was unsurprisingly disturbed by the fact that the suggested video concept was a three-minute animated cartoon starring Britney as a pink Power Ranger action figure. 'It would have been so embarrassing... so we came up with the idea for setting it in a school.' Britney wanted the video to reflect what the song was about and was trying to appeal to people of her own age so they could relate to it. The video, directed by Nigel Dick, was shot in two days at the familiar venue of California's Venice High School (Rydell High in *Grease*), was choreographed by Randy Conner and featured Britney in a skimpy school uniform – short skirt and white tied-up shirt.

Britney didn't have to look too far for some of her actors; the teacher in the video is actually her 'on the road' guardian and the guy who plays her love interest is her cousin! When the video was screened on the cable TV channel The Box, the station was overcome with calls for a repeat showing. On MTV it has been one of the most requested videos.

Since Britney's initial success, scores of offers have flooded in for her to make appearances on long-running TV shows and chat shows. Britney went back to the Disney Channel for their hit *The Famous Jett Jackson* and appeared as herself in an episode called 'Ghost Dance'. On the show she sings *Baby One More Time* at the high school's Halloween Dance. Britney also agreed to appear on *The Jay Leno Show*, a chat show which only takes the top names in showbiz (featured the week before Britney's appearance were Kevin Costner and Mel Gibson).

One of Britney's favourite guest appearances has to be in an episode of *Dawson's Creek*, 'It was weird because I watch the show all the time.' The episode was shot in New York and Britney was not willing to say whether there was any romance involved in the scenes, but did admit that her favourite character on the show is Pacey.

Britney's other TV credits include: *Good Morning America*, *NBC Christmas In Rockefeller Centre*, *The 1999 Billboard Music Awards* and *Nickelodeon's Holiday Help-A-Thon 99* to name but a few.

Britney enjoys a good comedy and they don't come much funnier than *The Simpsons*, on which she was pleased to make a guest appearance last year. However one show Britney is unlikely to sign up for is *South Park*. After watching one of the episodes, she was not impressed and found it offensive and sacrilegious.

Time Out With Britney Spears was launched in November of 1999 and is Britney's debut home video. In it, we see the true Britney at home and behind-the-scenes footage on tour and at video filmings. It's a classic every true Britney fan should have in their collection.

Being such a natural entertainer, it's not surprising that the idea has been put to Britney of making her own show. She has in fact already made a pilot episode and her lawyers have agreed a deal with TriStar. Britney quite fancies the idea of a young *Beverly Hills 90210*, however there are no plans to go ahead with a series just now. 'At the moment I'm concentrating on my music, but I want to do it in the future.' Now that's certainly something to look forward to...

THE BRITNEY CHALLENGE

Who wants to be a Britney billionaire? Sorry, no prize money is involved... but certainly if you make it through our Britney challenge you can hold your head high. Turn to page 44 for the answers and find out if you make the grade.

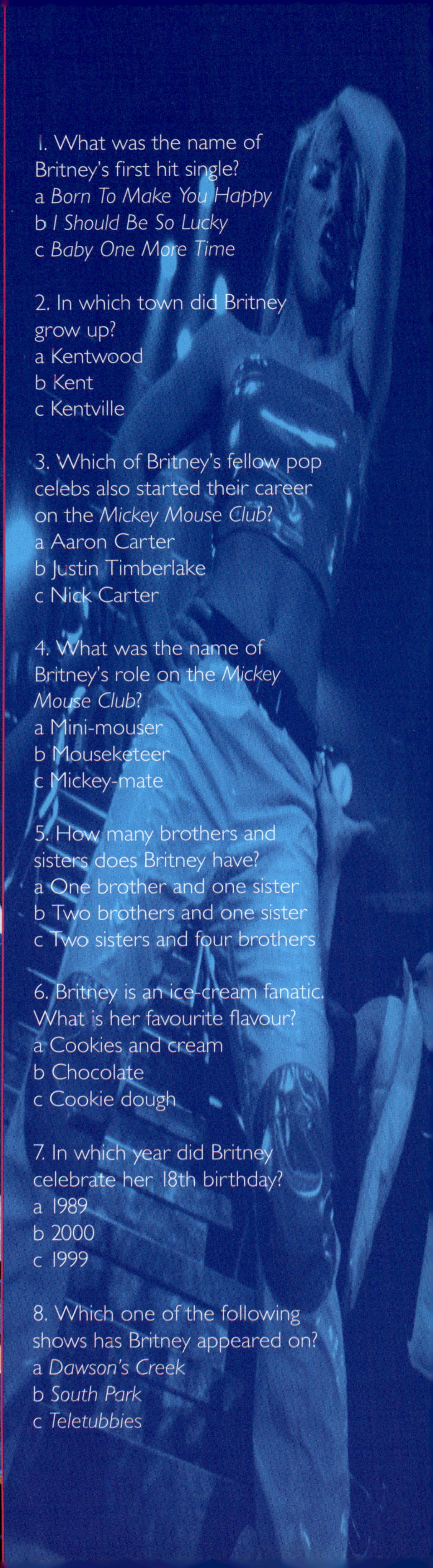

1. What was the name of Britney's first hit single?
a *Born To Make You Happy*
b *I Should Be So Lucky*
c *Baby One More Time*

2. In which town did Britney grow up?
a Kentwood
b Kent
c Kentville

3. Which of Britney's fellow pop celebs also started their career on the *Mickey Mouse Club*?
a Aaron Carter
b Justin Timberlake
c Nick Carter

4. What was the name of Britney's role on the *Mickey Mouse Club*?
a Mini-mouser
b Mouseketeer
c Mickey-mate

5. How many brothers and sisters does Britney have?
a One brother and one sister
b Two brothers and one sister
c Two sisters and four brothers

6. Britney is an ice-cream fanatic. What is her favourite flavour?
a Cookies and cream
b Chocolate
c Cookie dough

7. In which year did Britney celebrate her 18th birthday?
a 1989
b 2000
c 1999

8. Which one of the following shows has Britney appeared on?
a *Dawson's Creek*
b *South Park*
c *Teletubbies*

9. What is Britney's favourite colour?
a Lilac
b Blue
c Pink

10. Britney toured with which boys in the early days of her career?
a JC, Justin, Lance, Chris, Joey
b Kevin, AJ, Howie, Nick, Brian
c Ronan, Mikey, Stephen, Keith, Shane

11. When Britney recorded *Baby One More Time*, the song originally had been planned for someone else. Who was it?
a Aaron Carter
b Mariah Carey
c Backstreet Boys

12. In which sport was Britney a success as a child?
a Swimming
b Gymnastics
c Netball

13. If Britney was a Spice Girl, which one would she choose to be?
a Scary
b Sporty
c Baby

14. Where did Britney record most of her first album?
a Sweden
b Denmark
c USA

15. Which job does Britney think she would probably be doing if she wasn't a pop star?
a Bee keeper
b Dance teacher
c Music teacher

STRAIGHT FROM THE HEART

Being in the public eye means Britney has the opportunity to reach a massive audience, whether it be helping a good cause or speaking on topics close to her heart. She certainly stands as a role model for thousands of teenage girls and Britney understands this responsibility. Here we take a look at the issues that concern Britney...

HELPING OUT

November 1999 saw Britney join the TV channel Nickelodeon for a charity *Help-a-Thon*. Along with stars Mariah Carey, Elton John and 'N Sync, Britney donated her time at the 6th annual event which aims to promote volunteering by young people. The event helps over 20 charitable organisations, including Habitat for Humanity and March of Dimes. During the party, children from all over America called to pledge volunteer hours to help their community.

BEWARE YOUNG TALENT

Britney is concerned for young performers about age nine or ten who are already touring. At such a young age, apart from obviously being exhausting, the decision to go on the road was undoubtedly taken for them and may not necessarily be what they want. So beware...

EDUCATION RULES

Britney joined other celebrities for a national classroom reading campaign called Read for 2000. Thousands of students were encouraged to read for 2000 seconds at the same time on 10 December 1999. Showing her commitment to education, Britney supported the campaign by posting photographs and messages of encouragement on the scheme's website.

YOUNG LOVE

Britney has a mature attitude to romantic relationships. She knows all too well that falling in love at an early age can have its dangers. 'People can change so much,' she says. What does she feel about taking the relationship further? Britney can only advise, 'If you do meet the right person, you should wait until you are sure you really love him.'

GIVING SOMETHING BACK

In collaboration with The Giving Back Fund, Britney has formed The Britney Spears Foundation. Their first project is a performing arts based summer camp for underprivileged children, in the state of Massachusetts. The camp enables 100 children from urban areas in the US to spend two weeks attending free arts workshops and classes. Britney is delighted to be able to give something back to her fans, 'It's exciting to be able to inspire talented kids and help them pursue their dreams of performing.'

POSITIVE THINKING

Britney is privileged to have so much talent but she does work extremely hard – in fact much harder that she ever expected! She is keen to point out that anyone who has a talent musn't let it go to waste, 'If God has given you a wonderful talent for singing or dancing, then go for it... go for your dreams and what you believe in.' So, be confident and who knows, you could one day experience Britney's success!

SUCCESS IN STYLE

Voted 'most beautiful' in her high-school yearbook, Britney is used to getting a lot of admiring looks. But, like everybody else, Britney says she works at looking her best. She keeps her complexion clear by drinking lots of water, eating well and getting as much sleep as possible – not always easy with a hectic touring schedule!

With high energy levels necessary for performing complex dance routines, Britney works out to keep her stamina up and body in shape, making sure she doesn't overdo it, especially after a critical knee injury in March '99. Part of her routine includes calf lifts, stomach crunches and squats.

As soon as Britney had achieved her first number one slot, it wasn't only the American music fans who had taken notice. Designer Tommy Hilfiger asked her to be the 'Tommy Girl' in his new advertising campaign and ever since, Britney has received rails and rails of his clothes. Britney says her mum and sister are certainly not complaining, they're continually decked out in designer gear!

Britney loves to keep up on the latest style news and collections hot off the catwalk. She admires the work of designers such as Betsey Johnson, Calvin Klein, Donna Karan, Giorgio Armani and Bebe at XOXO. One of Britney's pastimes is shopping, so there's never a problem finding something in the wardrobe! At celebrity bashes and the numerous awards ceremonies that she is invited to, Britney loves to dress up, but usually keeps a classic and simple style.

For most of us, our first glimpse of Britney was in school uniform in the video for *Baby One More Time*. It was an image Britney came up with herself. 'I thought it was great because lots of kids could relate to it.'

Now rated one of the sexiest women in pop, Britney laughs remembering her Mouseketeering beginnings. 'I guess it started with that first video, although we didn't plan it to be sexy. It was shot in LA and so it was hot and people tend to wear less clothes!' Britney says her family are cool about her videos even though some people think they're a little too raunchy! Britney says, 'If people want to think I'm sexy, then I'm flattered. There are lots of different perceptions of sexiness.'

In order to reach her older fans, Britney has appeared in magazines like *Rolling Stone* and *FHM*. Britney appreciates how her style changes to suit different occasions. Though just to keep Britney's professional image in check, at every photo shoot there is a team casting their eyes over every piece of clothing and every photograph before anything goes to press.

There is equal consultation over Britney's stage clothes. She has her own stylist and clothes are carefully considered for each set. Britney enjoys working with the team and regularly comes up with her own ideas.

Taking time out of the public eye, there's nothing Britney likes better than hanging out at home in sweat pants and t-shirts. For casual comfortable clothes, Britney heads straight for Abercrombie & Fitch, one of her favourite stores.

HOME SWEET HOME

For Britney, home is definitely where the heart is. She says if she didn't enjoy her work so much, she'd probably be homesick all the time.

The town that Britney comes from is small... very small. In fact, the population of Kentwood is only about 1,200. That means that almost everybody knows of Britney and her success. When she goes home, which she tries to do about every six weeks, Britney says, 'Everyone's really sweet... everybody knows everybody there!'

Britney made sure that she spent that all-important millennium night at home with her family and friends. And when she couldn't make the Grammy Awards, Britney held a pyjama party in honour of the event at home with her mates!

Britney regrets that she doesn't get as much time as she'd like to meet up with her oldest and closest friends. Of course when there is time, they all like to go on a massive shopping spree together. While she's away, Britney makes sure she keeps in touch by phone, hence her massive phone bills, and by e-mail. She realises the importance of not forgetting old friends, because they are the true ones who knew her before she grew famous and aren't only interested in the fame. Yet one of Britney's mates who has her own fair share of fame is Danielle Fishel, who stars in *Boy Meets World*.

For her 18th birthday, Britney invited all her old friends from Kentwood for her party. She also invited lots of celebrities – not for her own sake, but because she knew her friends would love it!

Although she wouldn't swap her career for anything, Britney says certainly the worse part of fame is being away from family so much. Even bubbly Britney gets tearful sometimes when she's tired and of course the one she turns to is Mum. Britney says she calls her up all the time and often late at night, saying how much she misses her.

Britney's family has always been very close and supportive. Her parents don't fit into the typical showbiz mould and have always given Britney room to develop for herself. They certainly keep her feet on the ground and when at home for Britney has her fair share of household chores! Her Mum is a teacher and is like one of her best friends – they often have a girly giggle together, while Britney's Dad works in the construction industry. Britney has one brother and one sister, but there is no sibling rivalry in this particular household. Britney describes her brother as 'overprotective but cool' and clearly adores her younger sister, Jamie Lynn.

Britney takes care of her younger sister and is protective, especially when record companies are offering her a record deal at age eight! Britney's response is basically back off and 'let her live her life'!

Britney recalls one of her best childhood memories as the day Jamie Lynn was born. Britney was ten when her little sis entered the world and eagerly she asked to hold the baby in hospital. Much to Britney's horror, Jamie Lynn howled the minute Britney took her – so she swiftly passed her back. Britney chuckles when she remembers asking her Dad if they could give the baby back as she cried too much!

Childhood was pretty regular for Britney. Even when she was performing at the age of nine, it was only at weekends and the rest of the time she was hanging out with her friends like all other girls. 'I really didn't miss out... I had an amazing childhood!' she smiles.

TIME FOR LOVE?

Britney loves to be romanced. However, right now, she is happily single. 'I'm too busy to get serious with anyone, I'm happy to hang out with my friends.' That's not to say she doesn't believe in juggling a relationship and a career. Hard as it can be, especially with all the publicity that goes with the job, Britney believes it is possible. 'I think you can work hard and play hard... but you must enjoy every moment together.'

Britney hasn't missed out on young love by any means. She remembers her first kiss with a boy called Mason. 'I was fourteen and it just happened one day while we were watching TV at a friend's house.' Unfortunately for Britney, who says she had a major crush on the guy, the next day he ignored her – big mistake!

With an older brother, Britney was never short of male company or prospective boyfriends when she was younger. She says now that she's famous, they no longer ask her out on dates and are just friends. Some years ago however, it was a different story when Britney met her brother's friend Reg. She remembers with great fondness her first

boyfriend and first love. Reg was eighteen and Britney just fifteen at the time. 'It was really sweet when it happened,' she reminisces. Two years down the line however, Britney's career was making progress and of course she made the move to New York. 'We thought we'd be together forever, but he was happy in Louisiana and we were growing into different people... so we grew out of love!'

When you're the hottest thing in the charts, rumours of romance inevitably start, especially with other band members. Britney has been linked with Justin Timberlake and also Nick Carter. Britney says she's sorry to disappoint all the gossips, but there's definitely no romance on either count. 'Justin's still the same, sweet guy I knew when I was eleven and all the Backstreets are fantastic – but we're just great mates.'

Given all the attention Britney gets from being in the spotlight, it's often difficult to initially sort out the 'real men' from the boys, in other words, the trustworthy from the scandal-mongers. Britney says when it comes to romance, someone who doesn't care about the pop business and her being famous is more likely to win her heart.

Britney believes in love at first sight, although she admits so far she hasn't experienced it! So, what kind of man is likely to make Britney go weak at the knees?

'I like a tall man with nice eyes and a good smile.' Ben Affleck seems to fit Britney's bill. She's always quick to mention his name, and that of Brad Pitt, when it comes to naming her ideal man. Britney also wants her ultimate man to be confident, independent and 'someone who'd give me their undivided attention... and of course make me laugh!'

FACING THE FUTURE

The future looks bright for Britney and she's certainly not short on ambition. When asked what the next few years hold, she aims high, 'Maybe a couple of Grammy awards... my dream is to be a legend like Madonna!'

In showbusiness, you can be a hot name one minute and down on your luck the next. At the start of the Millennium Britney admitted that it would be a hard act to follow the success of 1999. She needn't have worried, 2000 simply added to her acclaim as a recording artist and her global recognition grew.

When Britney is asked the inevitable question of where she sees herself in ten years time, she is adult in her response. 'I simply want to grow as an artist, continue what I'm doing now, improve and appeal to a wider audience.' Britney's maturity is born from beginning her career at such an early age and surrounding herself with adults. She clearly knows what she wants. 'I've been told that I have an 'old soul' but I'm not serious all the time and sometimes I just don't care.'

"I want to be an artist that everyone can relate to"

It's hard sometimes to take in just how much Britney has achieved in such a short space of time. As a measure of her success, Britney has formed part of lectures at the International Association for the Study of Popular Music held at Middle Tennessee State University. Under the title 'Don't Stop Til You Get Enough: Consuming Popular Music' contributions to the music industry were discussed from Bob Dylan to TLC and Britney. 'I already have the success and stardom that I always wanted, so now I must go further.' One suggestion is producing records. 'I would love that,' she responds, 'but it takes a lot more experience... maybe in a few years.'

Something else Britney is keen to do in the future is a TV show, something like a young version of *Beverly Hills 90210*. Time however is the key and at the moment Britney wants to focus on her music. As part of a forward-looking future, she has invested wisely in a London home as her European base. Having success in England is very important to Britney as she now sees it as a second home.

So where would Britney be if she had not fulfilled her dream? One guess is back at home working as a dance teacher. Britney has said if her luck was down, she would more than likely go back to college. However she sees her destiny in performing, 'This is what I'm supposed to do... I'll probably stay doing this for the rest of my life...'

Looking way ahead, Britney's hopes indicate how important family is to her. Ultimately she says she would like to find the man of her dreams and live happily ever after with lots of children of her own. But that's a long way off...

Her advice for the future to her fans? 'Go for your dreams and live each day to the fullest!'

THE BRITNEY CHALLENGE ANSWERS

1. c - *Baby One More Time*
2. a - Kentwood
3. b - Justin Timberlake
4. b - Mouseketeer
5. a - One brother and one sister
6. c - Cookie dough
7. c - 1999
8. a - Dawson's Creek
9. b - Blue
10. a - JC, Justin, Lance,Chris, Joey
11. c - Backstreet Boys
12. b - Gymnastics
13. c - Baby
14. a - Sweden
15. b - Dance teacher

So, would you be a Britney billionaire?

If you scored
15 points: You certainly would be on your way to Vegas loaded up with cash. You really know your stuff. You're not a relation of Britney's are you?

9 - 14 points: A quick night out is all you're going to afford. Gem up on your Britney knowledge and have another go... a true fan never gives up.

Under 9 points: Don't spend your pitiful winnings all at once... there's not much to go around! Call yourself a Britney fan? I would get reading if I was you...

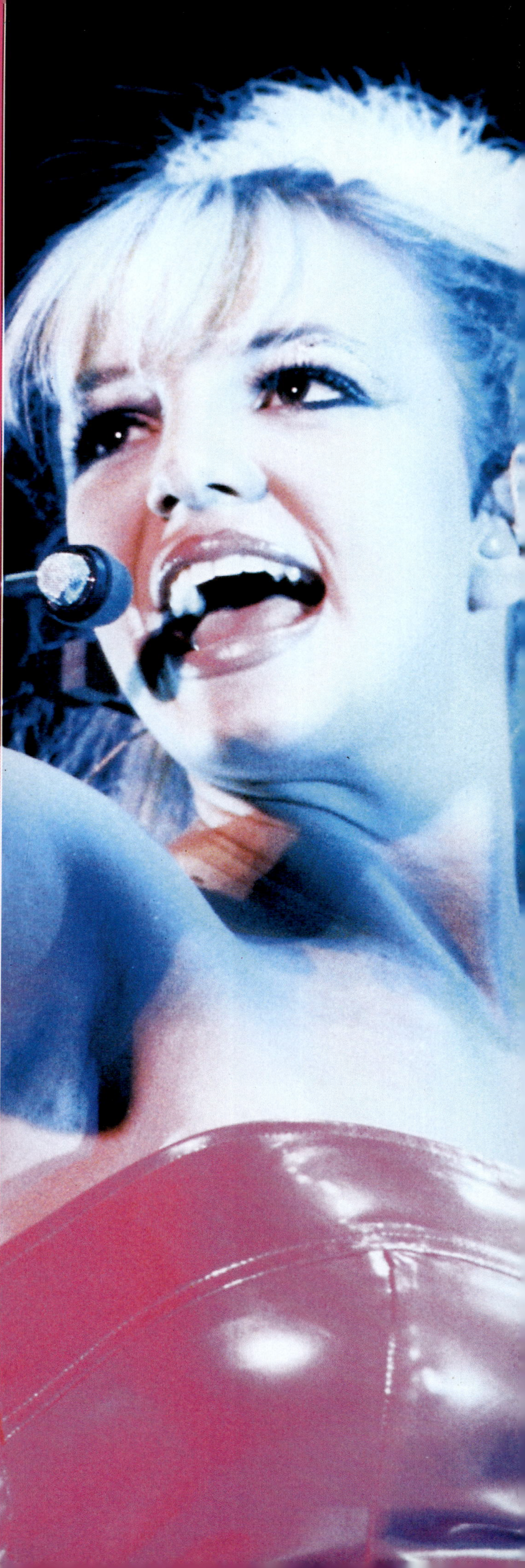

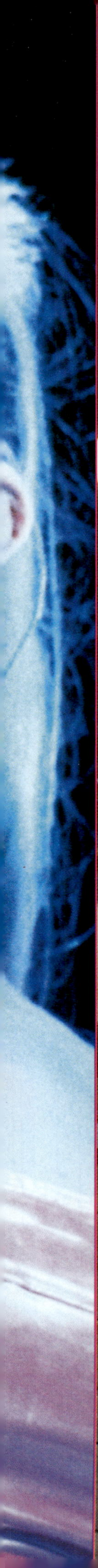
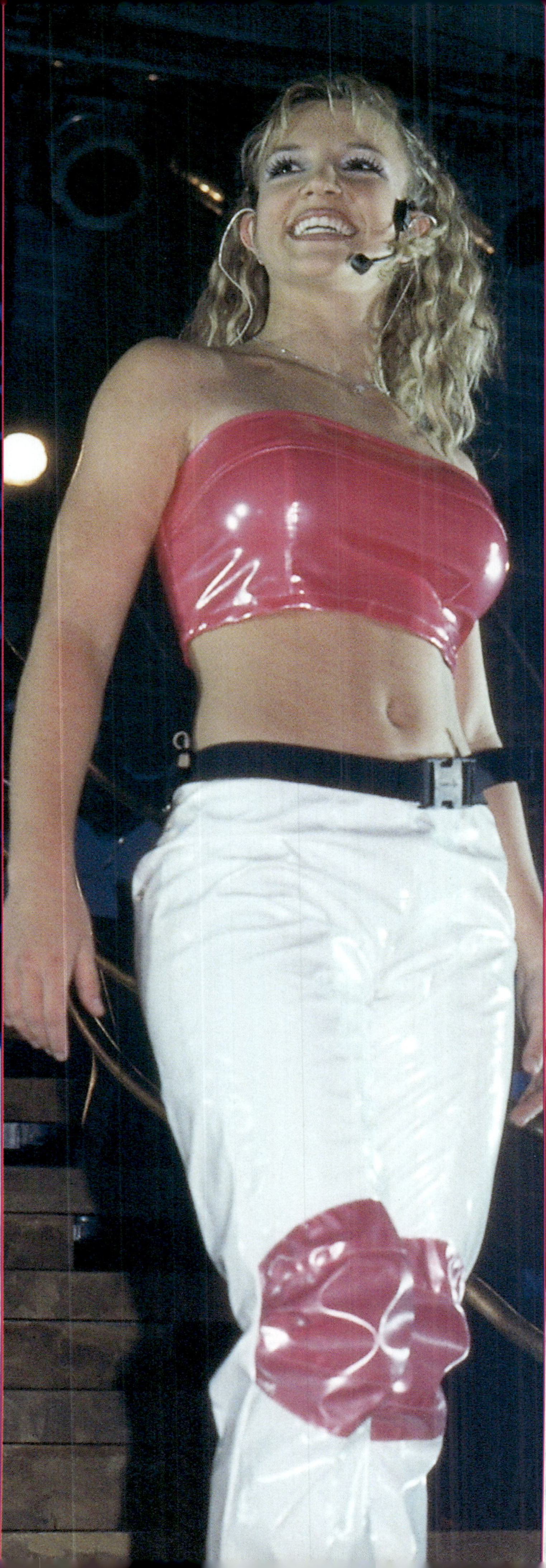
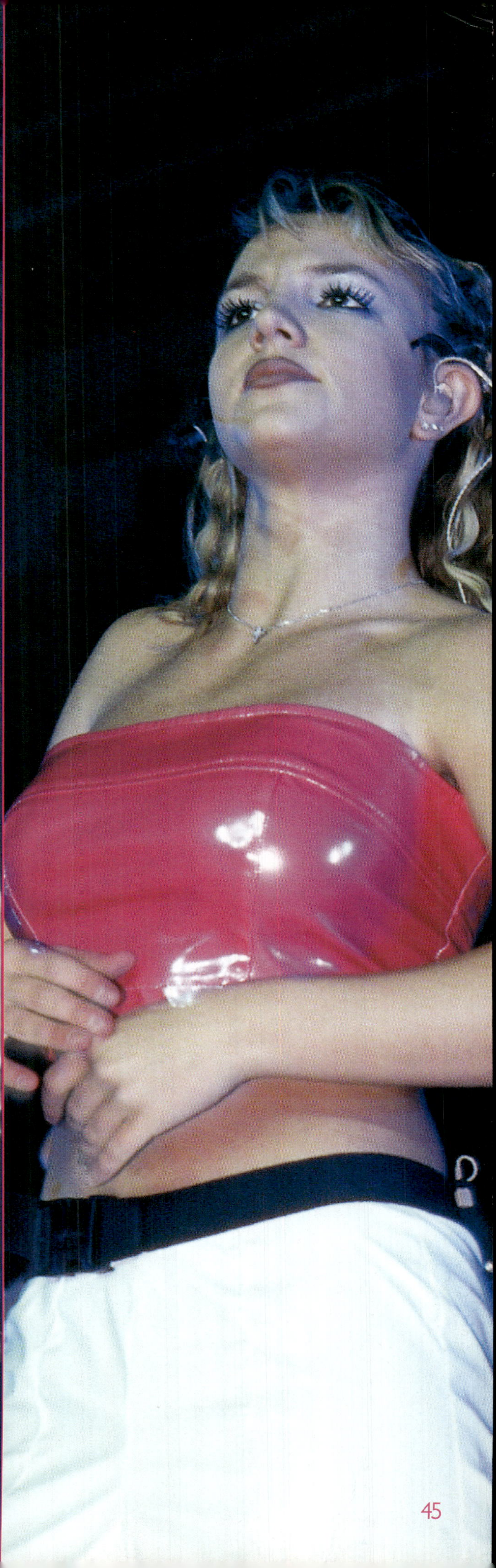

Britney

THE TOTALLY 100% UNOFFICIAL SPECIAL